Poems Old and New
1918-1978

Poems Old and New
1918-1978

by Janet Lewis

This is the poet's prayer,
That, summer being done,
You may find garnered here
Some leazings of the sun.

SWALLOW PRESS
OHIO UNIVERSITY PRESS
CHICAGO   ATHENS, OHIO   LONDON

Swallow Press Books
are published by
The Ohio University Press
Athens, Ohio

Library of Congress Cataloging in Publication Data

Lewis, Janet, 1899–
    Poems old and new, 1918–1978.

        I. Title.
PS3523.E866P64   811'.52   80-26209
ISBN 0-8040-0371-8
ISBN 0-8040-0372-6 (pbk.)

To Yvor Winters,

Now, as then

The author wishes to make acknowledgment to the following publications where some of these poems originally appeared: *Poetry* (Chicago), *Broom, Voices, The Forge, The Gyroscope, The Magazine* (Beverly Hills), *The American Review, The New Republic, The New Yorker, The New Mexico Quarterly, Twelve Poets of the Pacific* (New Directions), *The Wheel in Midsummer* (Lone Gull Press), *Manikin,* (Monroe Wheeler), *The Southern Review, The Ohio Review, The Compass* (University of Alberta, Canada), *Yankee,* Libretto for *The Last of the Mohicans* (Wilmington Opera Society), *The Ancient Ones* (No Dead Lines Press), *The Gramercy Review.* "Geometrics" was published as a broadside by Joseph and Joanne Dermont. *The Indians in the Woods,* from *Manikin,* has been reissued by Matrix Press.

Table of Contents

Introduction

The poetry of Janet Lewis collected here ranges over a period of sixty years. From the earliest poem included, "The Freighters" (which won her entrance into the Poetry Club at the University of Chicago in 1918) to one of the latest "*Paho* at Walpi, May, 1977," richness of intelligence and centrality of human concerns have characterized her poetry.

The earliest poems, 1918 to 1927, include a sequence on Ojibway Indian themes reprinted from her first book, "The Indians in the Woods," published by Monroe Wheeler in *Manikin* (1922)—the first booklet in a series in which hers was followed by those of William Carlos Williams and Marianne Moore. Written in free verse and Imagistic in technique, they anticipate slightly but thematically her historical narrative, *The Invasion: A Narrative of Events Concerning the Johnstone Family of St. Mary's* (1932). It is no coincidence that the American Indian consciousness—by which one might almost say that she is haunted, except that perhaps it is we who haunt the landscapes in which they more integrally lived—re-emerges as a theme in her recent verse, the seven poems beginning with "Kayenta, Arizona, May, 1977." The Indian consciousness with its intimate relationship to the natural world, its dependence upon the changing seasons, and with its ordered understanding of the basic experiences of birth, marriage, passion, death, evil and good, has an affinity with her intelligence.

First viewed from without, despite the internalizing devices of the experimental Imagistic movement, in these earlier poems on Indian themes, this characteristic consciousness begins to be explored from within, when, in the next group of poems, beginning with "Lost Garden," she turns to themes drawn from her own daily life and to forms long available in the English and American poetic tradition that permit use of the "I" (and "we") as well as the eye. From this period are three of her finest poems: "The Reader," "The Earth-Bound," and "Love Poem"—all from *The Wheel in Midsummer* (1927). "The Reader," though influenced by Imagistic technique, employs a rhetoric that is not limited to the clear, hard impression, but can express the relationship of sensory perception to conceptual experience more directly. This relationship is the specific concern of "The Earth-

Bound" (almost an *ars poetica*), where she defines the need for the sensory metaphor—"The flesh of our celestial thought"—to convey our understanding of conceptual matters—"the heavenly argument" —and also of "Love Poem," where the sensory perception carries the entire weight of the statement—but the direct statement is there, nevertheless. "The Earth-Bound" also, it should be noted, has her characteristic irony—often so gentle that it goes unnoticed.

Beginning with the poems written after 1928, when she first came to live in Northern California, two other important themes appear: time and death. "Time and Music," from the period 1928-1930, is one of her most impressive poems. Defiant in its elegant balancing of the conceptual and the sensory, it stands as the first of several poems (the latest, "The Drum" and "The Chord") that explore the problem of change and stability in terms of music's capacity to order experience—its power, like poetry's, to contain both life and death, as well as beauty. In music, time is the condition that gives being itself to the music, for time is both the "substance and the breath" of music, even while it is the "death" of—provides the end for—melody, the ordering principle. Analogically, she sees the human being, like melody, move through time. Artistic mimesis, whether in music or poetry, is of the ordered repetitions perceived in reality.

This concern with music, time, and, especially, with death as themes is continued in the group of poems written during the Depression and war years, 1930 to 1944, a period during which she also wrote a novel of contemporary life, *Against a Darkening Sky* (1943), several short stories collected in *Goodbye, Son* (1946), and the historical novel, *The Wife of Martin Guerre* (1941). The results of her poetic meditations on time and death show best in a poem on a new theme—birth—in the firm command of style and subject in "Child in a Garden: III," one of her best poems. The conceptual resolution is still expressed fully in sensory terms:

> The poplar bough, its plumes unbanding,
> The humingbird in thin air standing—
> Motion and quiet reconciled.

During this period, although time and death still preoccupy her as themes, the drive is toward balance—to "bind despair and joy / Into a stable whole"—in life as well as in music and art. In style, the poems of this period are all in traditional or nearly traditional prosody.

The last group of poems, written after an interval of many years, during which she published two historical novels, *The Trial of Sören Qvist* (1947) and *The Ghost of Monsieur Scarron* (1959), includes one of her best: "For the Father of Sandro Gulotta"—a culmination of her preoccupation with the themes of time, death, and birth. In execution it is a faultless handling of the themes. Composed on request and concerning a boy she did not know, this poem draws upon sources of feeling far beyond the immediate occasion. She does here something that she approaches doing in several earlier poems, but never quite so successfully as here: she captures the apparent simplicity of the child's life through the metaphor of the day lily. The lily functions as a paradigm for all the formal organizations of time (hours, days, seasons, years, etc.) that structure individual existence and that in structuring it grant lastingness. The dying child is seen only as alive, both in the day lily to which he is likened and in the "children" called from their play. Time as a form, as measure, is itself timeless and unchanging; it can take various embodiments, giving structure to them. In its rhetoric and prosody, this poem shows a grasp of the finest modes of English verse that seems both instinctive and learned. The organization is that of the "meditation," as practiced by seventeenth-century devotional poets. The precision of sensory detail, the use of the mixed anapestic and iambic measure, and the slightly archaistic "westering" recall Hardy at his most skillful, while the feeling is altogether different from Hardy. In the last stanza, the father is addressed, and the question asked suggests that his consolation is that Time itself may be perfectly fulfilled in a short as in a long period of life—already a classical *topos* when Ben Jonson wrote, "And in short measures, life may perfect bee." But here the implication is that formal structures, such as time exemplifies, are self-completing; and children, grasping instinctively this principle of order—of beginning, middle, and end—grasp a kind of immortality (a completed whole) in the short space of their "rounded day." Janet Lewis herself says this explicitly in "The Ancient Ones: Betátakin:"

> We do not recreate, we rediscover
> The immortal form, that once created,
> Stands unchanged
> In Time's unchanging room.

And also in "*Paho* at Walpi:"

> The sunlight pours unshaken through the wind.

To have seen and understood so much that is central to human experience and to have contained the understanding in enduring poetry is Janet Lewis' art.

—*Helen Trimpi*
1978

1918-1927

Northern Michigan and Santa Fe, New Mexico

The Indians in the Woods

Ah, the woods, the woods
Where small things
Are distinct and visible,

The berry plant,
The berry leaf, remembered
Line for line.

There are three figures
Walking in the woods
Whose feet press down
Needle and leaf and vine.

The Wife of Manibozho Sings

He comes and goes;
There is no rest
While he is here
Or gone.

I cannot say
That his feet have pressed
The leaves
He was standing on.

He comes and goes
And the maple leaves
Lie still
Under the sun.

The Grandmother Remembers

Ah, the cold, cold days
When we lived
On wintergreen berries and nuts,
On caraway seeds.

The deer went over the grass
With wet hooves
To the river to drink.

Their shadows passed
Our tent.

Nightfall Among Poplars

As light grew horizontal,
I, among bracken,
Felt the cold ripples
Among bracken stems.

The quick dry spider
Ran across my hand.

A Song for Following Gulls

Over the sand hill
I follow these;
They and their crying
Change like the seas.

I cannot tell you
What they have cried,
But the place of their going
Is empty and wide.

I follow creeping,
Tender and slow,
Watching the sand drift
Change as I go.

The Old Woman Alone

The Grandmother picks her way
Among the stones, the stones.
She passes deer.

Upon brown flanks
The balsam needles fall.

Ah, stranger than a deer
Caught in the open sunlight,
The old woman.

Manibush
and the Grandmother

With keen ankles
Dividing weed and weed
He shakes the dry seed
From the grass.

Fox feet, and five
Bare leather paws
And small sharp claws
Accompany him.

From the blue spruce
Tree where the wind blows
I watch the flashing
In the grass.

He Goes Away Again

In thorny juniper
The wind is cold,

In thorny juniper.

Shadows
Of stones grow white with evening.

The deer, the deer
Among the withered asters.

The spider,
Making tight her web.

Like Summer Hay

Like summer hay it falls
Over the marshes, over
The cranberry flats,
Places where
      the wild deer lay.

Now the deer leave tracks
Down the pine hollow; petals
Laid two by two, brown
Against the snow.

Anishinabeg
in the Cranberry Swamp

Autumn bows
The headed grass
With frost
And narrowed stem. Hoarfrost
Has rutted the swamp.

Their baskets fill
With berries green as water,
Their fingers cut
With searching the hard grass.

Boats gather
At the point of land,
Deep hulls
Beneath the swing
Of wide red sails.

They beg old quilts
And blankets,
Wake at morning
Frost from hip to shoulder
Like morning mist.

One Sits in the Woods

Gradual, continual approach
Of some one through the woods,
But no one comes.

The thin flame
Shoots up
Among grasses.

Violets, color of stone,
Minute and scarce
Where the great ants climb.

Exodus at Evening

Light came sideways
Into the hole;
The badger's children
Creeping sideways out.

Down they went
To bushes in the valley,
Treading silky yarrow.

Ojibway Village

Among grey cones
Odor of sweet grass
And warm bodies;

Burnt fish, about
The lukewarm stones,
And ash.

And the night, like ice,
Cuts color and odor
Like flowers under a sickle.

These bodies, so still
In the deluge
Of fine air.

The Rocky Islands

There are wolves
Cracking dry bones
On ledges
Among sweet gale bushes.

And at night
I climb to meet them
Over the light
Still flakes of rock.

The Threshing Wind

Cold and clear weather,
And the wind harries us
With a continual
Beating of the grass
For some fine seed.

The wild rice
Draws out its pointed leaves
With a perpetual flickering
As of wings
Or minnows turning.

These hold
The hard brown husk
That Manibush beat out,
Drawing the sharp green leaves
Against his shoulder.

Indians in Spring

The nights were cold
And they came slowly upstream,
Pulling past channel stakes
Gnawed white with ice.

Poplar flowers,
Blossoming and falling
Through air remaining cold
As water, the flesh of spring.

Sucker and Perch and Pike and Small-Mouthed Bass

Scavenger of the sunny beaches, I
Meditate and carry
Fish cast by the water,
Now paler than stones.

This night the skunk
Will retreat unappeased
With sharp feet and his airy tail.

He will not harry
Small fins
Grown whiter and thinner
Than foam.

Lost Garden

Children asleep in deep meadows.
Young popples
Grew round the house
And a wasp nest hung in the door,
Silvery like logs.
Garden mint and sweet william
Lost in the flowing grass.
Granny Cadotte, Granny Cadotte,
Your garden is running away!

Girl Help

Mild and slow and young,
She moves about the room,
And stirs the summer dust
With her wide broom.

In the warm, lofted air,
Soft lips together pressed,
Soft wispy hair,
She stops to rest.

And stops to breathe,
Amid the summer hum,
The great white lilac bloom
Scented with days to come.

The Wheel in Midsummer

The white roving
In my fingers,
Thread drawing thin.

My mother kneels
Beside the oven,
Lifting bread,

Her gold cross shining.
Hover of leaves
About the roof.

The Reader

Sun creeps under the eaves,
And shines on the bare floor
While he forgets the earth.

Cool ashes on the hearth,
And all so still save for
The soft turning of leaves.

A creature fresh from birth
Clings to the screen door,
Heaving damp heavy wings.

Cradle Song

Sleep, my baby, my own,
Canst hear the little wheel turn?
Canst hear thy mother a-baking and making
The butter come bright in the churn?
And sweeping and singing alone?

Sleep, my little, my dear,
The children are gone to the fair,
The farmers are gone to the clearing, and shearing
The little wee sheep with white hair.
So sleep, my little, my dear.

The Manger

What is the sweet savor?
Of hay? Of the swarm
Of hot-headed clover
Brought home to the barn?

The cattle are bending.
Their breathing is warm
As summer unending.
Ah, hush in the storm!

Ah, Child in the grasses,
Whose light spreadeth sure
And soft on the rushes
Laid over the floor!

The Tennis Players

Their flying feet are swift
And silent, and the lift
Of shoulder and of arm
And body without weight;
And radiant with charm
They play beyond the gate
Upon the shadowed lawn.
See how the vapors blow
From smudges on the lawn!
Indifferent and slow,
Light changes at the dawn
Of night in northern spring.
See how the players wing
About the tightened net!
White ball light in the air
From the far court to the near . . .
Dreaming I watch them yet
Across a continent.

The Freighters

I know what little cabins
The passing freighters see,
I know what pines and balsams
That sing unceasingly,
That sing with moving branches
Songs of eternity.

The buoys on the river
That turn and wink and turn;
I know the open places
Where the big brush heaps burn;
In sun the purple fireweed,
And in the shade the fern.

The water from Superior
Comes downstream lock and lock,
The wahbah-wayway honking
In a three-cornered flock,
And the red sails of Indians
At Molly Johnson's dock.

The leaves fall with the summer,
And after comes the snow.
The cabins like white canvas tents,
I know them, oh I know.
And up Saint Mary's river
The dull red freighters go.

Remembered Morning

The axe rings in the wood
And the children come,
Laughing and wet from the river;
And all goes on as it should.
I hear the murmur and hum
Of their morning, forever.

The water ripples and slaps
The white boat at the dock;
The fire crackles and snaps.
The little noise of the clock
Goes on and on in my heart,
Of my heart parcel and part.

O happy early stir!
A girl comes out on the porch,
And the door slams after her.
She sees the wind in the birch,
And then the running day
Catches her into its way.

Going Home from the Party

I heard the far lowing
Of cattle, homeward going;
I heard the wind slowing
In thick-leavèd bush;
I heard the quiet growing
Like leaves in the hush.

I heard the laughter fading;
Compliment, gay upbraiding
Into the quiet shading,
Night rising around;
Sunlight and daylight fading
Upon the air like sound.

I heard the deft passing
Of small creatures tracing
Night paths, and erasing
Day paths from the ground,
And the silence, deep-massing
In low-lying mound.

The Candle Flame

I feel myself like the flame
Of a candle fanned
By every passionate claim,
Flickering fast,
Or brought to an upright stand
In the curve of a hand.

There is nothing certain, nothing steady
About the mind
That can so alter and wind
Itself in sorrow and mood,
And be ever ready
To change like the leaves in a wood.

And what of our loyalty?
That would turn, alas,
To a flickering vagrancy,
The shadow of grass,
Were it not for the certain ever-recurring calm
Of the unknown sheltering palm.

The Earth-Bound

Still grove and hill and shadowy grot,
The flesh of our celestial thought,
Trammel the mind, however bent
Upon the heavenly argument.

The spring of wisdom ever flows
Pure shining water as it goes
Over the rocks and through the grass
Whither we stoop to hear it pass,

And healing is a tree whose leaves
Fall round us like the falling sleeves
Of love, that bending down at night,
Covers with them a face alight.

Tangled with earth all ways, we move,
And sleep at last in heaven that is a grove.

Meadow Turf

Goldenrod, strawberry leaf, small
       bristling aster, all,
Loosestrife, knife-bladed grasses,
       lacing their roots, lacing
The life of the meadow into a deep embrace
Far underground, and all their shoots,
       wet at the base
With shining dew, dry-crested with sun,
Springing out of a mould years old;
Leaves, living and dead, whose stealing
Odors on the cold bright air shed healing—
Oh, heart, here is your healing, here among
The fragrant living and dead.

Love Poem

Instinctively, unwittingly,
I came unto your hand,
For it dispenses quietness
With graciousness as grand

As the daughter of Demeter
In shadowy croft or glen
Dispensing sleep eternal
To tired working men.

The harvester lays down his scythe;
And lays his basket down
The vintner, and his heavy head
In vineyards overgrown.

Helen, the Sad Queen

Azure, 'tis I, come from Elysian shores
To hear the waves break on sonorous steps,
And see again the sunrise full of ships
Rising from darkness upon golden oars.

My solitary arms call on the kings
Whose salty beards amused my silver hands.
I wept; they sang of triumphs in far lands,
And gulfs fled backward upon watery wings.

I hear the trumpet and the martial horn
That wield the rhythm of the beating blade,
The song of rowers binding the tumult.

And the gods! exalting on the prow with scorn
Their ancient smile that the slow waves insult,
Hold out their sculptured arms to my sad shade.

From the French of Paul Valéry

During Illness

Ah, Landor, if thy page lay clear
For me these uneventful days,
Great courage I might study there,
Even Alcestis' quiet gaze.

To Walter Savage Landor

Captious old man, pass on
Through mounting ills of age;
Through death, then quiet find
Such as thine own great page.

May in the Desert

The dove of Jesus turns
Her colubrine sweet throat
Where the soft color burns
And pulses to her note,
Mourning,
And drawing down the sky
To stony earth,
Where the faint voices float.

Deer Dancers at Santo Domingo

The glowing shadows descended
Arroyo and arroyo,
But before morning
Lights ran, cries leapt,
The deer ran down the shadows
Upon painted sticks.

When the sun rose the deer
Danced upon painted sticks
In the sandy plaza.

Women came in silks, in cerise,
In white boots like the earth
To watch them.

A deer turned his head
Stiffly.
His horns were tipped with down.

1927-1930

Palo Alto, California

Time and Music

"Here. Trapped in Time."—Y.W.

Time, that gives to music life,
Measuring the motion's strife,
Time, the substance and the breath,
For melody is Time the death.

The melody upon it rides
Like fisher's boat upon the tides,
Or like the swallow through the air—
And vanishes while flying there.

And we, like music, through it move,
Or, lost from it, unqualitied,
From life as well as death are freed
And no design nor beauty prove.

"Here, trapped in Time," but Time for us
Both snare and breath and motion is.

For Cézar Franck

The D-Minor Symphony

The air is soft, a legendary haze, and far away
The sounds of spring are muted. Acre upon acre
The white trees, cut into here and there
By graveled roadways, scent the quiet air,
Lift up their cloudy fragrance into heaven.

Carolus Magnus sits beneath the trees.
White is his beard, white as a flower his hair.
The paynim and the Christ, the right and wrong,
Are legendary too, and far away.
Cézar, the horn, the violins, your instrumental song,
Are, like the spring, nostalgia for all these.
The music scents the heart like almond trees.

Country Burial

After the words of the magnificence and doom,
After the vision of the splendor and the fear,
They go out slowly into the flowery meadow,
Carrying the casket, and lay it on the earth
By the grave's edge. The daisies bend and straighten
Under the trailing skirts, and serious faces
Look with faint relief, and briefly smile.
Into this earth the flesh and wood shall melt
And under these familiar common flowers
Flow through the earth they both have understood
By sight and touch and daily sustenance.
And this is comforting;
For heaven is a blinding radiance where
Leaves are no longer green, nor water wet,
Milk white, soot black, nor winter weather cold,
And the eyeless vision of the Almighty Face
Brings numbness to the untranslatable heart.

Hymns by Firelight

Now the sweet cloudy voices rise and fall,
Blurring the soft damp air with melody,
And one sits shadowy with the white shawl
Drawn to her throat and folded over her knee,
Repeating gently the cadence of the hymn;
And the thick ash mantles the dim coals,
And the dew gathers on smooth leaf and stem.

Where they are sitting the firelight gleams
On their familiar faces, touching with charm
Or fantasy all the lines and seams
That the mind may have made, but the heart dreams,
Comforted, cradled and warm,
In these old words, cradle of many souls;
And the white ash gathers, heavy upon the coals.

White Oak

I grow forever in one place, yet stir abroad,
Flinging my small hard leaves upon the air,
Forever stirring in the air yet not
Forsaking this one spot.
All day along my trunk and branches hum
The motions of my life, and at my fingers' ends
The bright leaves dance.
Yet quietly I stand as in a trance.
In a long revery of life I stand
Like Him who stirs forever in His thought,
Yet moveth not,
An image of Him in my constancy,
An eldest child of God, the white oak tree.

Yet do I crumble, yet do I waste away,
Even as I grow. My root,
Five hundred years ago
Sunk in the earth, in this impoverished ground
Meagerly searches out
The tide that once did flow,
A permeating love, a music without sound.
My branches rot, my small twigs break and fall.
The owl, the hawk,
Find houses in my hollowed stubbornness.
Here is division, here,

That brings my endless stirring unto naught.
The green leaf and the sere
Hang side by side.
Ah, who has flung
These galls of death into the flesh of life!
Ah, who derides His thought!

Lines to a Kitten

Morsel of suavity
Perched on my knee,
Furred silken beast, your golden eye
With its great crystal lens is bent
Upon a fly
Six feet away, and all your tiny life, intent,
Crouches and peers through the dark slitted vent.

Only the great
And you, can dedicate
The attention so to one small thing.
Kin of philosophers, and more, indeed,
Kin of the fur and wing
From whose intensity we read
Abstractions, elemental thoughts, of fear or speed—

You, by your narrowed thought, maintain your place,
Pure quality of your great treacherous race.

Baby Goat

New-born, gilded with blood,
In the cold grass you lie,
And the sheened silver flood
About you falls away in ripples evenly.

All flesh is grass, indeed, my little goat,
But no grass pulses so with secret heat,
And no grass struggles so
To stand at once upon four staggering milk-white feet.

Your colorless clear eye
Turns here and there from person, shed and tree,
With such security as might declare
Here is the world at last and here am I.

O little creature, bloodily begun,
Still must you wear
Under your violet winter-leaf-like hair
The uncertainty of life where these warm currents run.

In vision presently
You'll merge with the dun coloring of grass and trees,
But you are none of these,
O colored like the summer-faded hill.

You are another race
Where pain's more evident
Negate this as you will,
And lift your brown and white complacent face,

Your little throat
With wattled ornament,
Into the spring's content,
Into the spring's chill silvery content.

47

Old Man

for Asa Smith

Silvered, beyond desire,
You ride the evening so,
Seated before the fire,
Your carriage robe the glow
Of fading coal,
The evening hour the measure of the mile;
The shades that flow
About your face the while
Less outward shadow than the inward shadowy soul.

Still wearing toward the dark;
A sixpence grown more dim;
And yet the sovereign's mark
In the deep-minted rim
Melts not away,
But rather grows more clear,
And more like Him
Who first affixed the year
And value to the silver-coinéd clay.

Or thus it seems to me.
Perhaps it only was
Your own nobility
Whose light deliberate pass
Has worn so fine
The coin; nay, more, then, printed the design.
In doubt I pause to trace
Against the moment's flight
The emblem of your face
Whose shadows still illuminate our night.

1930-1944

Santa Clara County

The Clock

Whose is the clock that strikes the hours,
    And strikes them true?
Above my beds of gaudy flowers,
    Of mint and rue,

The sound floats like a light that left
    A turning glass
To flicker along a wall, more deft
    Than hands that pass,

Having laid down the mirror's round,
    To coil soft hair,
Brushed on a summer morning, smooth
    To summer air.

Is it the clock we hid away
    Whose busy sound
Startled so loud our dreamy day,
    Cocoon-like wound,

And ever overlaid our lives,
    Mechanic, clear,
With ticking gossip of their lives
    Who first dwelled here?

Deep in the attic does it bide,
    Chatting alone,
By the warm rafter's roughened side,
    In monotone;

A heart, a recollection even,
    Of happy days
For those, since it was relegate to heaven,
    Gone sadder ways?

Or is it but some neighbor's clock,
    Some neighbor's, far
Across still fields, whose silver shock
    Floats the warm air?

Morning Devotion

In the fear of death I ask me
What is my heart's desire?
Here as I sweep the floor
And shade the sunny window
With what is it I task me?
Of heaven what implore?

Life to maintain and to increase
And to surround with peace
Like an orchard in sun
Where all's activity,
Leaf, earth and weighted tree,
Yet all resolved in one, one
Airy tranquillity.

And to maintain my soul
Content in this employ.
To bind despair and joy
Into a stable whole.
So day by day both house and spirit tending,
Feel all's complete at day's as at life's ending.

No-Winter Country

Her letters speak of trilliums, white
Beside the muddy water courses.
Cold spring, and then hot weather forces
Them suddenly north; they leave to-night.

And before I have more than thought of them gone,
There they are to the town returning,
And every note has a whiff of the burning
From brown leaves raked to a heap on the lawn.

A child grows tall whom I've never seen—
Precipitous seasons run pellmell.
They might be rumors out of a shell,
For has time gone by where I live serene?

I feel becalmed in an eddy of time,
Or shut by happiness, a great hill,
Into a valley of calm, and still,
These letters come from another clime.

Child in a Garden

I
O treasure! O joy!
The little sacred Boy
Upon His mother's knee
No sweeter was than she
Who now upon my heart,
Artless, and speechless,
Worketh with more than art.

Innocent flesh and frail!
The spirit's holy veil!
No older than the leaf—
Young April's first,
First herald of the sheaf—
That trims the poplar bough
With tremulous light,

Will you grow strong and tall,
O spirit infinite,
O body small,
Here where all things are growing,
And the spring air is blowing?
My heart is in your hand.
Grow tall and charm the land.

Child in a Garden

II
Sweet eyes that open to the sun
In gardens deep in bloom,
How curiously your tender gaze
Searches the pearly gloom,

The twilight mist of tree and bush,
Uncolored and unknown,
Where leaf and petal float the air
Bearing their shape, alone.

Soon will the haze grow softly bright,
With blue and gold anew,
The leaf with green, the rose assume
Her ancient lovely hue.

O born to miracles! The first
Must surely be this rise
Of rainbow and of summer dawn
To new-enchanted eyes.

Child in a Garden

III
It is the motion of the heart
That draws the slender lips apart,
Delight at life, the new-perceived,
The radiant, the many-leaved,
The poplar bough, its plumes unbanding,
The hummingbird in thin air standing—
Motion and quiet reconciled.
O smile again, sweet child!
All too soon these lips will be
With Hero's in eternity.

Lines to a Child

Dear child, relinquish your rich day,
With grace be parted from your joys.
Set orderly your lovéd toys
Upon the shelf in bright array,
And lay your gentle trusting head
Here, pillowed in your happy bed.

Come, sweetheart, come, and play no more.
Strange though this daily parting seem,
From light, from action, lost in dream
We learn what waking we ignore,
A peace all ills to benefit,
Wisdom beyond our conscious wit.

The nourishment of which you taste
Now as you close your eyes and sleep
Is dipped from a profounder deep
Than that with which our food is graced.
The limbs grow softly smooth and bright
That drink of it throughout the night.

My lot is shaped, like yours, my days
Toward an unwishéd sleep decline,
And sorrowing I must resign
All treasures, music, laughter, praise.
Come then, dear scholar, teach to me
The grace that makes compulsion free.

For Margaret Hamilton

who died August 31, 1933

I
The imagination, powerful to paint
The absent face upon the empty air,
And to make sound the floor below with steps
Hurrying with happy clatter to my stair.

Brings me again the laughter, the swift return
At noon of the child who haunts my heart, my day,
The return toward which the quiet morning moves,
And the steady sun with bright Time in his ray.

O gone forever, while joy mounts my stair
With staggering feet and high uncertain voice,
I remember your death, and with the same heartbeat,
The single beat, I grieve and I rejoice.

Be ever mingled with our happiness,
Dear vivid memory, often mount our stair,
And stand beside the living loveliness.
Beside her substance, paint your shadow there.

For Margaret Hamilton

II
You left no image of your face,
The firm contours, the lovely brow,
In ash destroyed, dissolvéd now
Save in the lines our memories trace.
And all your work was in that old
Symbol of our mortality,
The potter's clay, that, moist and cold,
Your fingers brought awhile to be
Fine vessels, platter, cup and bowl,
To hold like life the wholesome bread,
The milk, the wine. Ah, clear and whole
They stand and you alone are fled.

Fragile the monument! The glaze
You laid thereon, the blue and green
Like beetle's wings on sunny days,
An armor only to be seen,
Is no defense against the hour
When the hand, careless, shall destroy
The careful shape translated sure
From all that was your life's employ.
'Twas a right scorn for permanence.
These, not less lovely that the end
Implicit was in their design,
You lovingly spared no expense
Of care to finish, glaze and sign.
Yet signed mortality, sweet friend.

60

On an Old Woman Dying

Something was marred in making at her birth.
Neither the mind nor body prospered well.
In a short time the flesh was old and ill.
The child's intelligence, a childish mirth,
Halted its growth to live in that sad frame,
Life difficult and strange, and none to blame.

Unjust detention! Loneliness and pain
And ridicule pursued her all her days.
Yet in her speech and fierce bewildered gaze
The shyest child might read affection plain.
Daily she begged us to accept her love,
In charity to accept her and approve.

Now she is dying, and, half-blind with age,
The eyes peer dimly; now love may discern
Momently in their shades the gay return
Of courage, dissolution to assuage.
Let it be this in naming her we name.
This at her death may lasting radiance claim.

Lines with a Gift of Herbs

For Mollie Cohen

The summer's residue
In aromatic leaf,
Shrunken and dry, yet true
In fragrance, their belief,

These from the hard earth drew
Essence of rosemary,
Lavender, faintly blue,
While unconfused nearby

From the same earth distilled
Grey sage and savory,
Each one distinctly willed, —
Stoic morality.

The Emperor said, "Though all
Conspire to break thy will,
Clear stone, thou emerald, shall
Be ever emerald still."

And these, small, unobserved,
Through summer chemistry,
Have all their might conserved
In treasure, finally.

Carmel Highlands

Below the gardens and the darkening pines
The living water sinks among the stones,
Sinking yet foaming, till the snowy tones
Merge with the fog drawn landward in dim lines.
The cloud dissolves among the flowering vines,
And now the definite mountain-side disowns
The fluid world, the immeasurable zones.
Then white oblivion swallows all designs.

But still the rich confusion of the sea,
Unceasing voice, sombre and solacing,
Rises through veils of silence past the trees;
In restless repetition bound, yet free,
Wave after wave in deluge fresh releasing
An ancient speech, hushed in tremendous ease.

A Farewell

April, 1937

Here is no part
Of that we loved—
The tender heart
So quickly moved,
The wit, the laughter and the grace
Of gesture, the belovéd face.

Here is a vesture doffed:
White ashes, dim and soft.

In memory of her
Who could not be confined
Save in the loving mind
We scatter to the air
This precious residue.
O memory, be true.

Now blow, fair breezes, blow.
And go, dear ashes, go.

The April Hill

"She did not climb the April hill."
Aye, did she so,
But in no way
In which we're wont to say
Climbed she that hill.

She climbed a farther hill
More fair than show
The meadows here
Into an air more clear,
A light more still.

She climbed the April hill.
We saw her go
Clear in our view
Up to the edge of blue,
And upward still.

Music at a Concert

This is the many-mansioned, built in air,
The timelessly returning, built of time;
The only halls to which she may repair
Who long since passed beyond the reach of time.

Since she so loved this, ever I find her here
When men have laid their personal strife aside
That this impersonal grace may hold the air,
Whereby my loss is, for a time, denied.

The Hangar at Sunnyvale: 1937

Above the marsh, a hollow monument,
Ribbed with aluminum, enormous tent
Sheeted with silver, set to face the gale
Of the steady wind that filled the clipper sail,
The hangar stands. With doors now buckled close
Against the summer wind, the empty house
Reserves a space shaped to the foundered dream.
The Macon, lost, moves with the ocean stream.

Level the marshes, far and low the hills.
The useless structure, firm on the ample sills,
Rises incredible to state again:
Thus massive was the vessel, built in vain.
For this one purpose the long sides were planned
To lines like those of downward pouring sand,
Time-sifting sand; but Time immobile, stayed,
In substance bound, in these bright walls delayed.

This housed the shape that plunged through stormy air.
Empty cocoon! Yet was the vision fair
That like a firm bright cloud moved from the arch,
Leaving this roof to try a heavenly march;
Impermanent, impractical, designed
To frame a paradox and strongly bind
The weight, the weightless in a living shape
To cruise the sky and round the cloudy Cape.

Less substance than a mathematic dream
Locked in the hollow keel and webbéd beam!
Of the ingenious mind the expensive pride,
The highest hope, the last invention tried!
And now the silver tent alone remains.
Slowly the memory of disaster wanes.
Still in the summer sun the bastions burn
Until the inordinate dream again return.

A Lullaby

Lullee, lullay,
I could not love thee more
If thou wast Christ the King.
Now tell me, how did Mary know
That in her womb should sleep and grow
The Lord of everything?

Lullee, lullay,
An angel stood with her
Who said, "That which doth stir
Like summer in thy side
Shall save the world from sin.
Then stable, hall and inn
Shall cherish Christmas-tide."

Lullee, lullay,
And so it was that Day.
And did she love Him more
Because an angel came
To prophesy His name?
Ah no, not so,
She could not love Him more,
But loved Him just the same.
Lullee, lullee, lullay.

For Elizabeth Madox Roberts

Who died March 13, 1941

From the confusion of estranging years,
The imperfections of the changing heart,
This hour leaves only tears;
Tears, and my earliest love, Elizabeth, and changeless art.

To the Poet, Clayton Stafford, for His Verse

O measured line and sure,
The fact too hard to face
We cherish and endure
Through thine ennobling grace.

In the Egyptian Museum

Under the lucent glass,
Closed from the living air,
Clear in electric glare
That does not change nor pass,
Armlet and amulet
And woven gold are laid
Beside the turquoise braid
With coral flowers inset.

The beetle, lapis, green,
Graved with the old device,
And linen brown with spice,
Long centuries unseen,
And this most gracious wreath,
Exiled from the warm hair,
Meet now the curious stare—
All talismans of death.

All that the anguished mind
Most nobly could invent,
To one devotion bent,
That death seem less unkind;
That the degraded flesh,
Grown spiritless and cold,
Be housed in beaten gold,
A rich and rigid mesh.

Such pain is garnered here
In every close-locked case,
Concéntrate in this place
Year after fading year,
That, while I wait, a cry,
As from beneath the glass,
Pierces me with "Alas
That the beloved must die!"

71

Winter Garden

Child, dream of a pomegranate tree
Weighted with ruby, showered with gold,
Dream of a fig tree under the cold
And cloudy sky
Lifting its curved and silver boughs
Like a roofless house
For birds that be
Tardily in November here;
Dream of a spare
And twisted vine—
The grape—and ivy for the hair,
And honeysuckle, stubborn twine;
And of the firm and hidden shape
Of the green orange deep in the tree;
And dreaming, in my garden be.
    I have bestowed calendulas
That brighten beside reddening haws,
And rooted out the hoarhound grey,
And pulled the nettle from our way,
And torn my hand on bramble berry.
Then, if a drop, red as a cherry—
Bright blood—upon my finger show,
It is a seal set to a vow
To ward and to cherish even as now,
Now that you sleep your joy to replenish,
Each branch, each varied lifting bough,
That not a leaf in your garden perish.

Old Love

Love that is rooted deep,
Quiet as friendship seeming,
Secure as quiet sleep,
How many years redeeming
Your harvests keep!

Tears not in anguish shed,
The pulse's gentler motion,
Words spoken, phrases read,
The careful hand's devotion
Above the dreaming head—

Guard now the sleeping child
Whose nightly phantasy
With golden leafage piled
Plunders the fruited tree,
With golden fruit beguiled,

And guard the restless heart;
Visit with peace, discerning—
O love more wise than art—
How at late day returning
Those meet who need not part.

Helen Grown Old

We have forgotten Paris, and his fate.
We have not much inquired
If Menelaus from the Trojan gate
Returning found the long desired
Immortal beauty by his hearth. Then late,

Late, long past the morning hour,
Could even she recapture from the dawn
The young delightful love? When the dread power
That forced her will was gone,
When fell the last charred tower,

When the last flame had faded from the cloud,
And by the darkening sea
The plain lay empty of the arméd crowd,
Then was she free
Who had been ruled by passion blind and proud?

Then did she find with him whom first she chose
Before the desperate flight,
At last, repose
In love still radiant at the edge of night,
As fair as in the morning? No one knows.

No one has cared to say. The story clings
To the tempestuous years, by passion bound,
Like Helen. No one brings
A tale of quiet love. The fading sound
Is blent of falling embers, weeping kings.

Later Poems

1971-1978
Los Altos

For the Father of Sandro Gulotta

When I called the children from play
Where the westering sun
Fell level between the leaves
      of olive and bay,
There, where the day lilies stand,
I paused
      to touch with a curious hand
The single blossom, furled,
That with morning had opened wide,
The long bud tinged
      with gold of an evening sky.

All day, and only one day,
It drank the sunlit air.
In one long day
All that it needed to do in this world
It did, and at evening precisely curled
The tender petals to shield
From wind, from dew,
The pollen-laden heart.
Sweet treasure gathered apart
From our grief, from our longing view,
Who shall say if the day was too brief,
For the flower, if time lacked?
Had it not, like the children, all Time
In their long, immortal day?

Written for Vincenzo Gulotta of Milano whose son was dying of leukemia.

77

For Louise Chenery

July, 1971

Why did you wait so long
In the covert of the flesh, the painful flesh?
The deer, hidden in the leafy thicket,
Desiring of all things most the fresh
Sweet turf of the meadow, the sod
Joyous with flowering grasses, hesitates,
Fearful, unseen, to be seen
In that emptiness of light.
So did you wait, so fearful,
And so longing, hunted of God?

For John Muir, a Century and More After His Time

I have seen those Indians in their birch canoes,
Menominees, in shallow lake or stream,
Threshing their wild rice. Through Wisconsin haze
I see the water gleam,
                    the small craft tilt,
And through the clustering stems
The small waves lap upon the glacial silt,
As John Muir saw them, years and years ago.
Or do I use
A borrowed memory, learned in my childhood days
From my Ojibway friends?
                   All that Wisconsin scene,
Familiar as my breath, lives when I choose
To look upon his page:
The muskrat nibbling where the alders bend,
The water plants that gave it summer forage,
Great cumuli piled against thunderous blues
Of summer skies; hepatica and faint anemones
That come before the sunlit woods are leafy;
Bronzed oak and fiery maple, all the gold
Of harvest where the summer ends;
                   all these
In memory, both mine and borrowed, doubly rich are grown,
Till I can hardly tell his treasure from my own.

Now the Sierra tree, the Sierra wildflower glow
Near polished granite, bright as is the snow
That hoods the mountains of Yosemite
In my remembrance. These I truly know
That I have seen with my own eyes, and yet
There merges with them an unreckoned crowd
Of things more richly seen, of farther heights
Than I have ever traveled; seasons strange
And dangerous moments on that stony range
That Muir was first to call the Range of Light;

Moments of wisdom and intenser sight.
And these I owe to one
Who built his campfire on the canyon rim,
Who woke at dawn, and felt surrounding him
The mind of God in every living thing,
And things unliving, from the snowy ring
Of peaks, to, near his bed, the smallest heather
Lifting a fragile head
                    to greet the sun.

December, 1972

*Written for the Christmas Concert at Stanford Memorial Church
on Friday, December 8, 1972*

Rosemary, bay and redwood spray—
I pray you, love, remember.
The hills are green, the skies are grey
Here in our mild December.
We bring our candles and our wreaths
In honor of a blessed day,
To praise and to remember.

The nights grow longer, and there breathes
A coldness from the rainwet earth
Like sorrow rising in the heart,
A grief from wrongs in which our part
Was sometimes active, sometimes less
In hatred and neglectfulness.
But we are ever sinful men.
Earth's heavy shadow hides our sun
As if all joy should be undone,
As if we and our race were run.

Still in such darkness once was born
The very love that moves the stars;
Star of our night, first flower of spring,
The Holy Babe of Christmas morn;
Who is eternally reborn
For us in our remembering.
Therefore, though sorrowing, let us sing
In praise of God's eternal joy,
And of that little Holy Boy.

Fossil, 1919

I found a little ancient fern
Closed in a reddish shale concretion,
As neatly and as charmingly set in
As my grandmother's face
In a round apricot velvet case.

Fossil, 1975

Changed and not changed. Three million years.
This sunlight-summoned little fern
Closed in a cenotaph of silt
Lies in my hand, secret and safe.
In quiet dark transformed to stone,
Cell after cell to crystal grown,
The pattern stays, the substance gone.
Changed and not changed. Three million years
The Spirit, ranging as it will,
In sun, in darkness, lives in change.
Changed and not changed. The spirit hears
In drifting fern the morning air.

Easter Laudate

Golgotha, sorrowful hill!
From earth to heaven went,
Through darkness, through stormy air,
That one cry of despair,
Eloi, Eloi, Lama sabachthani!
Darkly, the firmament
Dissolved in raging air.
Earth trembled.
The veil of the temple was rent.
Then all was still.

In a far garden in a holy land
Joseph of Arimathea sadly laid
In his own tomb the body of his friend,
His teacher and his Lord, the Crucified,
Whom Peter loved, whom Peter thrice denied,
And whom Iscariot loved but yet betrayed;

Shrouded the piercèd hands and feet, the wounded side.
With all his strength rolled close the heavy stone,
So sealed the tomb and left his Lord alone,
Late on a Sabbath Eve, the Passion's end.

In darkness on the first day of the week
Into this garden came at earliest dawn
Mary the Magdalene her Lord to seek,
And found an empty tomb, the great stone gone.

Then, as the morning quickened into light,
She heard a step upon the gravelled path,
And, turning, saw the gardener, as she thought,
Standing in shadow under the sunlit trees.

Then she, fallen upon her knees, and weeping, said,
"O Sir, if you have borne Him hence, tell me

84

Where you have laid Him," and the gardener said,
"Mary!" and she, in wonder, "Rabboni!"
In wonder and unbelief. But she departed in joy,
As He bade her, to comfort His friends.

When she had told her tale,
Not one believed, not one.

Oh, Love so sorely grieved,
So slowly known,
So tremblingly believed,
In sorrow and fear by His own folk received!

Laudate! Laudate!
Slowly the morning light
Climbs to the roof of the sky.
Laudate, laudate,
A thousand voices cry,
Under the vaulted naves of Christendom,
In humble chapels, or in lonely rooms,
Where a few are gathered together in His name,
Laudate,
Praising the Love that cannot die,
And hope undying, the rebirth
Of beauty to the living earth.

Lo, where the sunlight glows on the new corn,
Sunlight transpiercing the young April leaf!
Lord, I believe! Help Thou my unbelief!

"Mary," He said, and she, in wonder, "Rabboni!"

*Written for the music composed by Alva Henderson,
commissioned by the Heritage Program of Millsaps
College, Dr. Richard Freis, Director, October 1976*

Kayenta, Arizona, May 1977

I fall asleep to the sound of rain,
But there is no rain in the desert.
The leaves of the trader's little cottonwoods
Turn, turn in the wind.

The Anasazi Woman

I think of her so often,
The woman of the Anasazi, the Ancient Ones,
Who is the sun-dried mummy in the museum
In Tucson. Very small,
Shrunken incredibly,
She lies on her side, slightly curled
In a posture of childhood.
Beside her, her sandals,
Worn by her step upon the earth which stays,
Lies still, unchanged,
Beneath the dazzling sun.

A little woman, old in death, how old
When she first laid her on the earth to sleep?
Mother, grandmother, daughter
Beautiful with youth,
No one can tell, unless the anthropologists
Have searched her bones. But I,
Bent above her case,
Divided from her by the glass
And by how many centuries,
Think of the peace and splendor of her days;

How, unconfused, she met the morning sun,
And the pure sky of night,
Knowing no land beyond the great horizons
Of this spare, stony land,
But knowing well the pulse beneath the skin,
The living seed within her, and the seed
Which, honored and bless'd,
With her own hands she laid in earth
To rise again in corn.
Oh, knowing well
The touch of air and sun,
The constancy of earth, she named

87

In her own language
The gods of earth and air and water,
The gods of life,
Who are the One in many changing forms,
Names lost forever.

Oh, unconfused and bless'd,
In a strange sepulchre your body lies,
Most beautiful, most unconcerned, and small,
My sister, my friend.

The Ancient Ones: Betátakin

Time stays, they said. We go.
They moved through Time as through a room
Under the great arch of Betátakin.

We cannot hear their voices.
What words they spoke
To echo here, to rise along the walls
Of this steep canyon,
Are gone; and yet the jay,
The warbler speak their notes
And the wind blows, whirling the aspen leaves,
Brushing the thick short needles of these pines,
And by the path
The small flowers still are bright—
Vetch, bluer than turquoise,
Clustering white stars;
And all the leaves are new, early in May,
Small, perfectly shaped, each to its odd design,
And gleaming; and the porcupine
Climbs from his tree with easy slumberous grace.
His quills shine in the early light,
A halo, as he goes
Into the mist of green.

Time stays, the canyon stays;
Their houses stay, split rock
Mortared with clay, and small.
And the shards, grey, plain or painted,
In the pale roseate dust reveal, conceal
The patterns of their days,
Speak of the pure form of the shattered pot.

We do not recreate, we rediscover
The immortal form, that, once created,
Stands unchanged
In Time's unchanging room.

The Ancient Ones: Water

And did they too, the ancient ones,
Like the Navajo who now possess the land,
Have multiple names for water,
The changing one, without whose gift
Nor earth nor sun availed them?

The spring at the cliff below Betátakin,
The river that nourished
Wupatki, the long-deserted,
These doubtless had their names,
Being individual. But water itself,
How could they name it with one word?

Tsaile, Chinle,
Water flowing in, flowing out.

Still water caught in a pool,
Caught in a gourd;
Water upon the lips, in the throat,
Falling upon long hair
Loosened in ceremony;
Fringes of rain sweeping darkly
From the dark side of a cloud,
Riding the air in sunlight,
Issuing cold from a rock,
Transparent as air, or darkened
With earth, bloodstained, grief-heavy;
In a country of no dew, snow
Softly piled, or stinging
In a bitter wind.

The earth and sun were constant,
But water,
How could they name it with one word?

Shape-changer by whose power
Frogs, plants and men had life, apart
From sand and rock.

Water flowing in, flowing out.
Tsaile, Chinle.

Paho at Walpi

The prayer feather fluttered
In the wind that swept the prow
Of the First Mesa at Walpi, fluttered,
Caught in dried earth,
The trodden clay,
Under the great sky,

A bit of down, a thread of handspun cotton,
A twinned pine needle, small quilled feather,
Before a house with a padlocked door
In quiet of an early morning when
Most of the doors of the village
Were closed against
                the chill sweep of the wind;

A *paho,* carrying what supplication,
Or what gratitude,
Shaken in the wind which it entreated;
Perhaps.

The sunlight pours unshaken through the wind.
Carry my entreaty, also, fluttering feathers.

Awátobi

"This is holy ground," he said, our Hopi guide,
And he was right to say so; but I think
It was not sanctified for him
Because here died
Of Christian martyrs a great number.
Rather, because the dead remain,
Unquiet, unreleased,
His own people slain by his own people
In a holy war;

Men of Awátobi
Killed by men of the Three Mesas,
By arrow, by fire,
Betrayed, trapped in their own kivas.

After some dissension and some deaths,
The women and children were gathered
Into the lives of the Three Mesas,
To dance in the old ceremonials,
To honor the masked divinities.

It is old, the story of a holy war.

At Santo Domingo on the Rio Grande
Far from Awátobi, yet not so far
As to have been spared the Spaniard's cruelty,
On the Saint's Day now, the Saint
Sits in the plaza under a bower of green,
While the dancers,
Beautiful in dignity of pace and gesture,
Dance for him as well as for the Corn.

But at Awátobi, when the walls of the mission
Rose hugely above the cliff,

The men of the Three Mesas,
In terror for the peace of the great kachinas
Who hold the world together,
Who hold creation in balance,
Took council, acted.
After the holocaust
No one returned.

Perhaps some thieving of roof timbers
From unburned houses,
Perhaps some looting
When the women were led from their homes
Replenished dwellings of the Three Mesas.
Few Navajo or Hopi cared to risk
A meeting with the dead.

And as the years went by
The houses crumbled.
Only the anthropologist, learning
Of a ruin, untouched,
All but unvisited, altogether undisturbed,
Dared to intrude,
To lift the perishing frescoes
From the walls of the mission,
To gather a few fragments
Into the safety of a museum.

We look down on the hawk and the hawk's shadow.
The plain is wide. Whether desert, half-desert,
Ravined, at such a distance who could tell?
But the cloud shadows pass over it
With the shadow of the hawk,
And rifts of light change suddenly.

Somewhere under all this brightness of earth
Where we walk,

This dried grass beating in the wind,
These shards, with colors fresh as day,
Somewhere under our feet,
Choked with earth, stained with blood and ash,
Lie the kivas, the double heart of the village.

Blood in Paris, after the Saint Bartholomew,
Blood at Awátobi, for a cause so similar;
And it was only yesterday. In Time,
Less than three centuries.
Purcell was only lately dead. Racine
Living almost into the hour of the disaster.
Above the careful gardens of Versailles
Madame de Maintenon and Louis styled the Great
Dreamed of a single faith for France,
And the Huguenots of Nantes
Were fled to England.

The shard in my fingers is clear;
The design I have seen lately on a living pot:
The head of a serpent in black, an oval
Narrowed quickly behind the jaws,
The long tongue darting;
The very same. I leave it in the grass
With others.

The guide has come with us to protect
And interpret his inheritance,
Terrance Taliswaima, to whom
I dedicate these lines.

Whether he brought a small offering
Of great power, pollen,
And a pinch of blue corn meal,
I cannot guess. But he said,
"This is holy ground," and he was right.

Drum

There is a drum
In a museum north of Flagstaff,
The sides of wood,
The head of rawhide,
To be tuned by warming.

In that drum
Tied to a cord of rawhide
Stretched diagonally
From top to bottom
Is a buckskin bag,

And in that bag
Are the voices
Of all the best singers of the pueblo.

Where are they now, those singers?

Was that drum taken
From Awátobi after the great disaster?
Or from another pueblo, more happy?

When that drum
Shall be beaten again
How they will resound,
Those voices!

Lake George, on The Mohican

August 14, 1977

The rocky islands,
Layered and polished
By the fierce powers
Of cold and time,

Tufted with pine and cedar,
Shadow the moving water
With their old masonry,
Hold the half-hidden houses,
Lighted like fireflies,
Safe in this hour;

And in the summer evening darken,
Darken slowly above the shining lake,
As the boat moves forward,
The metal trembling slightly underfoot.
And time moves slowly.

The wind is gentle.
              We breathe the scent of water.
No sudden darkness. Slowly
The sunlight leaves the rounded cloud,
And dimly, in a great leisure,
The old constellations repossess the sky.

Time paused, and we moved into Time.
Two hundred,
      more than two hundred years ago,
Terror was on these shores,
But in our sheltered moment, all the anguish
Of that old violence was gone,
And sorrow yet to come remained unknown.

97

Carol for the Nativity

At His birth as at His death
A fearful darkness held the earth,
But bright His star and radiant host
Proclaimed the joy and not the cost.

How dark the earth since that far day!
Of broken stone, and rough, the way!
Guide us, fair star, the hard way home.
Sweet heavenly Child, Thy kingdom come!

The Chord

In a moment of grief, a word
Bringing happiness, bright
Beyond all dissembling
Struck like the heart of a chord,
Two notes that clung like lovers
And left me trembling.

Garden Note I, Los Altos

A spring storm shakes the old peach tree,
Making the branches glisten,
Scattering the dark petals,
While the cherry,
Young as any bride,
Holds fast her white clusters.

Garden Note II, March

Nothing more hesitant
Than the way the poplar seedlings take.
Nothing more certain than the intention
Behind their wanderings. They float
Over the grass, over the roof, and beyond
My garden, beyond this day,
As I saw them years ago,
On this same ground,
Under this same tree.

Snail Garden

This is the twilight hour of the morning
When the snails retreat over the wet grass
To their hidden world, when my dreams, retreating,
Leave me wondering what wisdom goes with them,
What hides in mouldering earth.

Softly they go, the snails,
Naked, unguarded, perceptive
Of the changing light, rejoicing
In their slow progress from leaf to stem,
From stem to deeper darkness.
Smoothness delights them.

What do they hear? The air above them
Is full of the sharp cries of birds.
Do they see? The lily bud,
Three feet above the soil on its leafy stalk,
Is known to them at midnight
As if it were a lighthouse. Before sunrise
They have gnawed it half in two.
Toothless mouths, blind mouths
Have turned the leaf of the hollyhock to lace,
And cut the stem of the nasturtium
Neatly, just below the blossom.

The classic shell, cunningly arched, and strong
Against the hazards of the grassy world
Is nothing before the power of my intention.
The larks, also, have had their fun,
Crashing that coiled shell on stone,
Guiltless in their freedom.

But I have taken sides in the universe.
I have killed the snail that lay on the morning leaf,

Not grudging greatly the nourishment it took
Out of my abundance,
Chard, periwinkle, capucine,
Occasional lily bud,
But I have begun my day with death,
Death given, death to be received.
I have stepped into the dance;
I have greeted at daybreak
That necessary angel, that other.

Hummingbird, Los Altos

I hear you in there, hummingbird,
In the thicket of the orange tree,
Whirring of wings, click of beak,
Furious intent assault
Upon the honeyed blossom.

You come from foxglove bells
In a garden overlooking a great river,
In a summer long gone.

But I deceive myself. The ruby-throat
Does not cross the Rockies.
You are perhaps an Anna. Suddenly
You leave the tree, spiral
Into a grey sky, turn
In horizontal flight,
And are gone.

In a Convalescent Hospital

I say, Lord, let her go.
Her flesh has melted underneath her skin;
The skin is bleached like leaves after the weight of snow
Slow winter month on month, mottled and shrunk,
And lined with swollen veins; her lips
Are fallen in upon her gums; and her white hair,
Grown thin as mist, lets show her skull.
Only her eyes are dark and bright,
And in a moment of full recognition, catch my gaze,
Full of surprise that I have come
Out of a day long passed, to bring my love.

I was a child and she was full of beauty,
Her long dark hair forever slipping from its combs.
By the low fire she laughed, and caught the coil,
And lifted it, still laughing, to her head,
And pinned it there;
The while my mother, smiling, chatted on,
Above the flutter of the little flames.

So well she sang! So patiently
From my embarrassed throat she coaxed a sound
Small credit to her patience. Still, she glowed,
Her eyes on mine, while her lips trembled
With the growing note
That from her own throat brightened, swelled,
And rounded, and grew dim. All this
To teach a troubled child to sing.

Now she speaks hurriedly,
In sudden panic clutching at my hand. Oh,
Let me out of here! Where am I? Here?
I don't belong here. Let me go!
And I? What can I say? Lord, let her go?
Yet who am I to say, Lord, let her go?

105

Why is she here, and why
Am I here with her to remember joy?
What can I know
Of gentleness engendered by her need,
Of charity bestowed
By those who never saw her young?
They come and go in rounds impersonal, prescribed,
Prescribed, and even paid for, yet are kind.

I take this moment for its preciousness,
In grief for her, for me,
And pray it bless
Both her, and me.

Geometries

Yaddo, North Studio, May 1979

I see a motion, not a form,
In the shaggy spruce beyond my window;
Beyond the diamond panes, the doubled triangles,
Trembling with morning light, I see
A branch trembling where there is no wind.
The bird has taken flight.
I close my eyes and see
The pentagon, which is
The morning-glory and the Christmas star,
Down whose dark throat
Thought travels and is lost,
Form lost in motion where
The guidelines for the bee converge
Upon ephemeral booty, beyond
Ephemeral blue.
How many seasons have I met
These morning faces?

The pentagon,
Braced against space,
All angles true,
Widening out from the square,
Ignoring the simple balance of the paired,
Uneven, and secure,
How it recurs!
In mountain laurel, apple bloom,
And the wild rose, invisible line
From petal tip to
Petal tip, the five
Doves of the columbine
About a fountain.
It recurs, a form, not a motion,
Flickering in time,
Assuming a meaning without substance,
Haunting Time.

The window pane, a diamond composed of four
Diamonds, shivering in the sun, two triangles
Enlaced becoming Solomon's star,
Doubled as in a mirror, becomes
The crystal snow,
The bee's damp cell,
Unsullied, pure,
As yet unfilled, in the new hive—
These famous hexagons!
I am bewildered with geometries. Pythagoras,
Say, what do you make of all this,—
These living forms, created, uncreated,
Returning, dissolving,
Haunting Time?

Words for a Song

Love is a constant
Like the speed of light,
Unbroken spectrum
Of the purest white,
Rainbow unbroken
In the beam of light.

Love is an anguish
That, gathering at the root,
Rises in sap along the rugged branch,
Pulsing in sunlight,
To lose itself in fruit,
To break in fragrance
Above the sunny ground,
Like wine in autumn,
Like insect wings unbound,
Like wings of gauze and rainbow.

Or so I dreamed.
Or so I found.

1980

First Songs for Night of Miracles

Mary

Slowly, slowly, Joseph kind,
Joseph gentle, kind and good,
Slowly, slowly must I go.
Forgive me that I lag behind,
So heavy have I grown, so slow.

Joseph

Mary gentle, Mary pure,
Yet a little while endure.
You will see your gentle Son
Very soon, very soon,
As the angel promisëd.

Mary

Joseph gentle, Joseph kind,
I know that He will heal the blind,
Console the dying, raise the dead,
Give His life for sinful men,
Die Himself, yet live again,
So the angel promisëd.

But so heavy is He now,
Only slowly may I go.
Sweet Son, Whose face I long to see,
Find me now a bed;
Only a quiet place to lie
Safe from the coldness of the sky,
And the angry eyes of men.

Songs for Cora

from the opera, The Last of the Mohicans,
composer Alva Henderson

I: On the Way to Fort William Henry

Green covers us.
Green leaves that screen us
From the summer sun
Let shine the sunlight through a brighter green.

God's wilderness surrounds us in a maze
Of leaves, of light, of fragrant air.
Evil, forbear.
Into this wilderness, trusting in God,
We dare.

II: In the Cave at Glens Falls

The falls surround us.
Our trail has been swallowed by the woods,
And carried away by the water.
Our struggles, our pain,
Our deep desire to comfort our father,
Become as nothing beside this rushing water,
These walls of living rock,
Ancient as Time!

We are lost in the heart of Time!
What peace to be so lost!
But we must go on.

The Wonder of the World

(for a choral piece by Alva Henderson, Autumn, 1979)

From the old stone
The carven words reproach me,
Beside the rows of quiet dead:

The wonder of the world,
The beauty and the power,
The shapes of things,
Their colors, lights and shades,
These I saw.
Look ye also
While life lasts.

Earth, air and upper air,
Earth, air and water I knew,
And the sun on my face.
The voices of women and men,
The shouting of children,
These I knew.
Harken ye, also.
Drink while life lasts
The wine of astonishment.

So spoke the stone.

> *The seven lines of the second stanza are taken from an old Swedish gravestone, and are quoted by Olaus J. Murie of Moose, Wyoming.*